YOUR ARMY OF DOLLARS

by Luisa Tennant

Archway Publishing books may be ordered through booksellers or by contacting:

Archway Publishing
1663 Liberty Drive
Bloomington, IN 47403
www.archwaypublishing.com
844-669-3957

Interior Image Credit: Joe Huffman

ISBN: 978-1-6657-2685-6 (sc)
ISBN: 978-1-6657-2684-9 (hc)
ISBN: 978-1-6657-2683-2 (e)

Print information available on the last page.

Archway Publishing rev. date: 07/14/2022

ARCHWAY
PUBLISHING

Acknowledgement:

For all the Children in the World.

During the course of your life, you will receive a whole army of soldier dollars.

These soldier dollars have a job.

Their job is to protect you from harm.

These soldier dollars are precious and willing to take direction from you for almost anything you want.

Right now you are a kid. But once you get an army of dollars, you will become a commander.

A commander must know what orders to give when he gets an army of soldier dollars.

He must learn to lead the way!

He must learn commands to make soldier dollars protect him for the rest of his life!

First we have to attract these little soldier dollars.

But how do we do that?

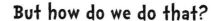

We do this by adding value to other people's lives!

To start, you can do chores for your parents!

4.

Sometimes you can do chores for a neighbor.

Whatever way you get little soldier dollars, it is because you made another person's life better!

6.

Imagine you earned a little army of 20 soldier dollars.

As a commander, you have to direct these little soldier dollars to do the right thing.

We are going to look at these commands and get your little soldier dollars to protect you for the rest of your life!

You are going to give the first 2 little soldier dollars orders to jump to your Forever Freedom Account.

At first those little soldier dollars will live in the jar. But as you add more little soldier dollars to that jar, you will order them to go to the bank.

There, those little soldier dollars will attract more soldier dollars And grow and grow and grow.

These dollars will stay with you for the rest of your life!

9.

The next 2 little soldier dollars are ordered to jump into your education account.

Little soldier dollars love people who know how to read and write.

It is also important to know your math!

When you are educated, you can help your little soldier dollars keep in line. Then they will want to help you for the rest of your life.

As the commander, you are going to order 2 more soldier dollars to march to charity.

Not everybody has 20 little soldier dollars like you.

You do not have to give everything you have, but it is good to give something.

This makes you a better person, and it will help make the world a better place.

Many commanders want something special in their lives.

But 20 little soldier dollars are not enough. So commanders must order at least 2 of their little soldier dollars to save up.

Like the forever freedom account, these 2 little soldier dollars will be joined by others until there is enough to get that very special item!

LONG-TERM SAVINGS

Then, with your parents' permission, feel free to buy it!

Now there are 12 little soldier dollars to order as you please!

Their job is to march to special places to make you happy!

15.

You and your friends can play video games!

ICE CREAM

Share ice cream cones with a friend!

17.

If there is not enough soldier dollars to do the things you want to do, you can put them into your play jar and save for events in the future.

When those dollars are joined with other dollars, you can do things that are more costly.

For example, you and your friend can spend a day at the slide pool!

Play miniature golf!

20.

Go to a movie!

While you are waiting to get enough soldier dollars to pay for the big event, enjoy the free stuff!

22.

Now we have to look at the rest of the story....

Someday you are going to be an adult.

Right now, you can order these 12 extra soldier dollars to do whatever you want to do.

But in the future, you will have to add 2 more jars.

LIVING ACCOUNT

TAXES

You must create a Living Jar.

After you have ordered soldier dollars to Financial Freedom, Education, Charity, Long Term, and Play, most of the rest of your soldier dollars will go to support you for the rest of your life.

LIVING ACCOUNT

Then you will have to order some of those soldier dollars to pay for the roof over your head, food on the table, heat in the furnace, clothes on your back.

They must help to keep you strong and healthy.

The next order you will give to your little soldier dollars will be to pay taxes.

Many people do not like to pay taxes.

But taxes are very important!

TAXES

Taxes pay for the policemen.

Taxes pay for firemen.

TAXES

28.

Taxes pay for garbage pickup.

TAXES

Taxes even pay for your country's army!

TAXES

Little soldier dollars that march to pay taxes help keep your country safe and clean.

By making other people's lives better, your little soldier dollars will come to love you and want to follow your orders.

If you treat your soldier dollars properly, they will do the best they can for you.

They will keep you warm and safe for the rest of your life!

May your army of dollars keep you safe and happy!

32.

Note to Parents
An Addendum
By Luisa Tennant

Your Army of Dollars teaches basic money handling to children. However, you as parents, know that there is more to the story. Especially when it concerns the Forever Freedom Account.

Once your children grasp the concepts of the jars, Introducing further concepts to them as they get older will help them create satisfying lives. They may even be able to go on adventures, and lead remarkable lives.

Even though taxes are important, it is also wise to keep them legally reasonable and not pay too much. That is why children should become familiar with the following arrangements.

Taxable Investments	Tax Deferred Investments	Tax Free
Stocks and Bonds	Traditional IRA's	Roth IRA's
Mutual Funds	401(k)s & 403(b)s	Permanent Life Insurance
Savings Accounts	Annuities	Municipal Bonds
Certificates of Deposits		College Savings Plans
Crypto Currency		

Whether you are a pro, or if you feel these are too complicated, it is good to know all or most of the above. Therefore, I encourage you to persuade your school to develop age-appropriate financial instruction throughout your children's education. Some schools are already doing this.

The more children learn to aptly handle money, the more the world will benefit.
You, as parents, would then be proud of the legacy you leave behind.

Printed in the United States
by Baker & Taylor Publisher Services